English for Retail Handbook

Eric Thomas

ISBN: 1522971661
ISBN-13: 978-1522971665

CONTENTS

Lesson 1
Greetings/Farewells in Retail

Greetings

Hello
How are you doing today?
Welcome to *Summer's*.
Good morning
Good afternoon
Let me know if you need anything.
Is there anything I can help you with?
How can I help you?

How may I help you?
What can I help you with?
Is there something I can help you with?
If you have any questions, please let me know.

Greeting Practice Dialogues

Sales Clerk: Hello. Welcome to <u>Summer's</u>. If there is anything I can help you with, please let me know.
Customer: Thank you. I will.

Sales Clerk: Good morning. Welcome to Summer's. Is there anything I can help you with?
Customer: Yes, I'm looking for a sweater.

Sales Clerk: Good afternoon. How can I help you?
Customer: I'm just looking. Thank you.
Sales Clerk: If you have any questions, please let me know.

Customer: Excuse me?
Retail Clerk: Yes? How may I help you?
Customer: Where are the shoes?

Customer makes eye contact.
Sales Clerk: What can I help you with?
Customer: Where is the bathroom?
Sales Clerk: It's over there.

Role Play

Split class into 2 groups. One group are the retail clerks. Another group are the customers. Customers come into the room and a retail clerk help greet them. Students take turns acting.

Farewells

Did you find everything you were looking for?
Thank you.
Goodbye
Have a nice day.
Have a good day.
Take care.

See you next time.
Thanks for coming in.

Farewell Practice Dialogues

Sales Clerk: Thank you. Have a nice day.
Customer: Thank you. You too.

Sales Clerk: Have a good day. See you next time.
Customer: Okay. See you. Goodbye.

Sales Clerk: Thanks for coming in. Take care.
Customer: Thank you.

Sales Clerk: Did you find everything you were looking for?
Customer: Yes. I did.
Sales Clerk: Great. Have a nice day. Goodbye!

Sales Clerk: Your total is 32,000 won.
Customer: Here you are.
Sales Clerk: Thank you. Would you like a receipt?
Customer: No, thanks.
Sales Clerk: Thank you. Have a good day.
Customer: Bye bye.

Role Play

Students split into two groups like "greetings" role play. Retail clerks say goodbye to customers as they leave the room.

Lesson 2
Simple Customer Requests

Warm Up

Write customer questions that you have heard:

- _____

- _____

- _____

- _____

- _____

Key Vocabulary/Phrases

out of stock
come in
check out
cash register
one size fits all
comes in one size only
sales tag / price tag

Typical Customer Requests

Could you help me?
I have a question.
Where are the *shoes*?
Could you tell me where the *fitting room* is?
Where is the *sales tag*?
Can I return this later?
Does this come in a *large*?
Do you have this in a *large*?
Do you have this in a *blue*?

Assisting the Customer

Let me check.
Let me find it for you.
Let me show it to you.
Come this way, please.

Practice Dialogues

Customer: Could you help me?
Retail Clerk: Yes. How can I help you?

Customer: Do you have this in a large size?
Retail Clerk: Yes. Let me check.

Customer: Do you have this in a medium?
Retail Clerk: No. I'm sorry. It's out of stock.

Customer: Could you tell me where the fitting room is?
Retail Clerk: Yes. Go straight and it is on the left.

Customer: Does this come in a large?
Retail Clerk: That is one size fits all.

Customer: Do you have this in a 28?
Retail Clerk: No. It doesn't come in 28. It only comes in a 30.

Customer: Where can I check out?
Retail Clerk: The cash register is over here.

Customer: Do you have this in a blue?
Retail Clerk: No, I'm sorry but we are out of stock. Would you like me to check for another color?
Customer: Yes that would be great. Do you have it in beige?
Retail Clerk: Okay, I'll check. No, I'm sorry. It doesn't come in beige.

Customer: Excuse me. Could you help me?
Retail Clerk: Yes, what can I help you with?
Customer: Do you have this in an extra small size?
Retail Clerk: Yes, we do. Let me find it for you.

Customer: Does this come in a small?
Retail Clerk: No, it doesn't. It only comes in one size.

Fitting Room Requests

Could you tell me where the fitting room is?
Where is the fitting room?
I'd like to try this on.
Where can I try this on?

Practice Dialogues

Customer: Where can I try this on?
Retail Clerk: The fitting room is over here. Let me show it to you. Come this way please.

(After trying on)
Customer: Where can I put this?
Retail Clerk: You can give it to me. Thank you.

Purchase Requests

Where can I check out?
I'm ready to check out.
Where is the cash register?
How much is this?
Where is the sales tag?

Practice Dialogue

Customer: Where can I check out?
Sales Clerk: The cash register is over here.

Customer: Excuse me. How much is this blouse? I can't find the sales tag.
Sales Clerk: Let me find it for you. It is 49 dollars.

Returns Request

Can I return this later?
What is your return policy?
Can I return this later if I don't like it?
If my husband doesn't like this, can I return it?

Practice Dialogue

Customer: Can I return this later if I don't like it?
Sales Clerk: Yes. You can return it but you should not remove the tag and bring both receipts with you. Also, you need to bring it back before 31 days and bring the credit card you paid with.

Activity: Students create their own dialogue using their company's return policy.

"Where" Questions

Where are the stairs?
Where is the elevator?

Where is the bathroom?
Where are the shoes?

Practice Dialogue

Customer: Excuse me. Could you tell me where the bathroom is?
Sales Clerk: Sure. Come this way, please. It's on the second floor.

Customer: Where are the shoes?
Retail Clerk: They are over there. Let me show you.

Lesson 3
Customer Preferences

Vocabulary

have *something* in mind
browse
try *something* on
in particular
something comes in _____ (size/color)
arrival

Key Phrases

Did you have anything in mind?
     Yes. I'm looking for *shoes*.
     No, I'm just looking./ I'm just browsing.
Are you looking for anything in particular?
     I'm looking for *jeans*.
Here are our new arrivals.
This is our new arrival of *floral skirts*.
Do you prefer *red or green*?
What type of *pants* are you looking for?
Those come in *black and grey washed* only.
Let me see if we have this in another *color*.
If you'd like, I can see if we have this in a *large*.
Why don't you try it on?
Can I help you with anything?
Let me see if we have it in another *color*.

Learning customer's preferences with questions

Sales Clerk: Are you looking for anything in particular?
Customer: No, I'm just looking.
Sales Clerk: This is our new arrival of denim jackets.
Customer: I like those. Very nice.

Sales Clerk: Can I help you?

Customer: No, I'm just browsing.
Sales Clerk: Did you have anything in mind?
Customer: I'm looking for jeans.
Sales Clerk: Do you prefer tight or relaxed fit?
Customer: I prefer relaxed fit.
Sales Clerk: Okay, let me show you these items.
Customer: What types of colors do you have these in?
Sales Clerk: Those come in black and grey washed only.
Customer: I prefer the grey washed. Thank you.

Learning a customer's preferences by giving options

Sales Clerk: Can I help you with anything?
Customer: Yes. I'm looking for a jacket.
Sales Clerk: The jackets are over here. How about these?
Customer: No. I don't like this kind of style.
Sales Clerk: We have a different selection over here.
Customer: I like this but I don't like this color.
Sales Clerk: Let me see if we have it in another color.
Customer: Yes! I love this very much in yellow.

Role play

Students seperate into groups of 2 or 3. Students act as customer or clerk and change roles for each situation.

Situation 1: Customer is just browsing. Find out what they like.
Situation 2: Customer is just browsing. Recommend a new arrival.
Situation 3: Customer is looking for something particular. FInd the one they want.

Lesson 4
Making Conversation

Key Phrases

Is there anything I can help you with?
What brings you in today?
Are you shopping for yourself or someone else today?
Did you have anything in mind?
Let me know if I can help you with anything.
If you'd like, I can show you some of our newest items.
Are you looking for anything special?
That would look great on you./That looks great on you.
What do you usually like to wear?
How about this *black skirt*?

17

This is very *fashionable/stylish* these days.
Is it a gift?
Do you want it wrapped?

Practice Dialogues

Browsing Customer

Sales Clerk: Is there anything I can help you with?
Customer: No thanks, I'm just looking.
Sales Clerk: Are you shopping for yourself or for someone else today?
Customer: Just shopping for myself. I saw the store and decided to come in.
Sales Clerk: Well, if you'd like, I can show you some of our newest items.
Customer: Yes, that would be great! Thanks.

A Customer Who Needs Something Particular

Sales Clerk: Hi, let me know if I can help you with anything.
Customer: Okay, I will.
Sales Clerk: Are you looking for anything special today?
Customer: Yeah, I am. I have these beautiful red heels, but I need something to match with it.
Sales Clerk: How about this black dress? It's very stylish these days. It would look great on you.
Customer: Okay. I can try it on. Is there anything else you can show me?
Sales Clerk: How about these grey-washed jeans?
Customer: Oh, yes. I prefer these than the dress. Let me try it on.

Customer Interested in Trying New Styles

Retail Clerk: Hi! Welcome to Jessica's. Are you looking for anything special?
Customer: No, not really. I want to find something new. I lost a lot of weight and I'm giving myself a little makeover.
Retail Clerk: That's wonderful! Well, did you have anything in mind?
Customer: I'm not sure yet. What would you recommend?
Retail Clerk: You can try on our latest style. Let me show it to you. It would look great on you.

Customer Shopping for Another Person

Retail Clerk: Hi, let me know if I can help you with anything.
Customer: Yes, I'm looking for something for my wife for her birthday. She loves Summer's. But I'm not sure what to buy her.
Retail Clerk: Okay. What does she usually like to wear?
Customer: She likes wearing dresses and heels a lot. I'd like to get her something warm since it's Winter.
Retail Clerk: Let's take a look at our newest sweaters. They are very fashionable these days.
Customer: No, I don't think that's her style.
Retail Clerk: Okay. How about our WInter coat selection?
Customer: Do you have this one in grey?
Retail Clerk: Yes, we do. Let me find it for you. Here it is.
Customer: Yes! She will love this! I'll take it.
Retail Clerk: Do you want it wrapped?
Customer: Yes. That would be great.

Role Play

Role play each type of customer with a partner. Use the worksheet. Then change partners and act without worksheet. Try to use your own words.

Lesson 5
Store Knowledge

Vocabulary

General Clothing Sections

- Men's
- Women's
- Children's
- Shoes
- Accessories

Retail Facilities

- Fitting/ Dressing Room
- Restroom/ Bathroom
- Stock Room

Check Out Counter

- Cash register
- Line
- Returns

Entrance/Exit

- Door
- Stairs
- Elevator/Escalator

Customer Questions

Could you tell me where the *fitting room* is?
Can you tell me where the *bathroom* is?
Where is the *cash register*?
I can't find the *stairs*.

Key Phrases

It's over here.
It's over there.
Let me show you.
I will show you.
Come with me.
You will see it on your right/left.
Go straight.
Keep going straight.
Turn right/left.

Practice Dialogues

Customer: Excuse me. Where is the *elevator*?
Retail Clerk: It is over there. Go straight. You will see it on your right.

Customer: I can't find the cash register.
Retail Clerk: Come with me. I will show you.

Customer: Can you tell me where the fitting room is?
Retail Clerk: Yes. Go straight. You will see it on your left.

Customer: Could you tell me where the Men's is?
Retail Clerk: Keep going straight and you will see it.

Lesson 6
Product Color & Size

Vocabulary

out of stock
come in a *size/color*
have in a *size/color*

Colors

Red	Purple	Green	Blue	Pink	Brown
Black	Orange	Beige	Grey	Striped	
White	Light Purple	Dark Green	Floral		
Neon	Flannel	Neon	Khaki		

Size

XS-----Extra Small
S----- Small
M----- Medium
L----- Large
XL----- Extra Large

Customer Questions

Do you have this in a *size/color*?
I'm looking for a *small*.

Key Phrases

What *size/color* are you looking for?
It comes in *size/color*.

I doesn't come in *size/color.*
Let me find it.
Let me look for it.
We're out of stock.

Dialogue Practice

Customer: Do you have this in a large?
Retail Clerk: Yes, we do. Let me find it for you.

Customer: Excuse me. Do you have this in orange?
No, I'm sorry. It's out of stock.

Customer: Do you have this in red?
Retail Clerk: No, I'm sorry. It doesn't come in red.

Retail Clerk: What size are you looking for?
Customer: I'm looking for an extra large.
Retail Clerk: I'm so sorry. It doesn't come in an extra large.

Lesson 7
Garment Care

Vocabulary

Machine Wash
Bleach
Line dry
Tumble dry
Iron
Dry clean

Tag Examples

Machine wash cold. With like colors, only non-chlorine bleach. Tumble dry low. Low iron. Do not dry clean.

Professional dry clean only.

Customer Questions

Customer: How can I take care of this?
How can I wash this?

*Usually cleaning instructions are written in other languages. If a customer asks, its better to show them the tag.

Activity: Choose two items you are wearing today. Write down instructions to clean it.

Lesson 8
Introducing Best Sellers

What are the Best Sellers in Your Department?

Make a list here:

1. _____

2. _____

3. _____

4. _____

5. _____

Vocabulary

best seller

Key Phrases

These jeans are our newest collection from Europe.
Would you like to see our new collection?

Dialogue Practice

Retail Clerk: Hello, may I help you?
Customer: Yes, I'm looking for some new jeans.
Retail Clerk: These jeans are our newest collection from Europe.
Customer: Yes, that is fantastic. I will try it on.

Customer: I'd like to see your most popular items.
Retail Clerk: Yes, would you like to see our new collection of skirts?

Lesson 9
Fashion Elements

Vocabulary

Classic
Fad
Spring/Summer collection
Fall/Winter collection
somebody is into *something* (somebody likes something)
come/have in

Customer Questions

Do you have your *Fall/Winter collection* in yet?
Do you have anything more *casual*?

Dialogue Practice

Retail Clerk: What kind of clothes are you shopping for?
Customer: I'm looking for a sweater.
Retail Clerk: Why don't you take a look at our Winter collection?

Customer: Excuse me, do you have your Summer collection in yet?
Retail Clerk: Yes, it just came in. What kind of item are you looking for?
Customer: I'm looking for a skirt.
Retail Clerk: Okay. What about this skirt? This is one of our best sellers.
Customer: Oh no! That's too showy! Do you have anything more modest?
Retail Clerk: Yes, we do in our classic collection. Let me show it to you.

Specific Styles & Product Terms

What are some styles you can find in your store?

_____

_____

_____

Preppy: *plaid skirts, sweater vests, pearl necklaces*
Punk: *skinny jeans, leather, studs, piercings*
Hipster: *ironic t-shirts, skinny jeans, vintage*
Modest: *covered up, long skirts, sweaters*
Sophisticated: *suits, trousers, pencil skirts, blouses*
Sporty: *sweats, t-shirts, tennis shoes*
Trashy: *way too "showy"*
Minimalist: *black, white, straight design*
Edgy: *converse, skinny jeans, black boots, basically some punk but not all punk*
Vintage: *older styles, like an old band on your t-shirt*
Western: *brown leather, blue, browns, and orange: cowboy boots and hat*
Nautical: *blue red and white, bows, and collars*
Beachy: *sandals, flowy sundress, sunglasses*
Futuristic: *metallic, what you imagine people in the future to wear*
Rocker: *band logos, kind of punk*
Boho-chic: *baggy shirts that go in at the bottom, big purses, casual, long necklace*
Flirty: *cute dress*
Casual: *shorts, short pants, flip flops/sandals*
Formal: *nice dress and heels*
Casual chic: *casual yet cute*
Hippie chic: *baggy clothes, peace signs, headbands worn around the head, bellbottoms, tie dye, bright colors*

Source:
http://answers.yahoo.com/question/index?qid=20090615163035AAVISrl

Activity: Groups of 3 or 4 people. Discuss about each person's style today and why they fit that style.

Key Phrases

What kind of style are you into?
Why don't you take a look at our new *sweaters* over here?

Dialogue Practice

Retail Clerk: What kind of style are you into?
Customer: I like beach style. A little bit hippie and casual.
Retail Clerk: Why don't you take a look at our new flower dresses over here?

Homework: Bring 3 fashion photographs you like to class. Describe the clothes and the style to the class.

Lesson 10
Fitting Room Service

Vocabulary

try on
sales rack
stockroom
check out

Key Phrases

How many items are you trying on?
Here is an open room.
I'll go check in the stockroom.
We have *skirts* that would go with that.
Would you like to see it?

Practice Dialogues

Retail Clerk: Hello. How many items are you trying on?
Customer: Two pants and one shirt.
Retail Clerk: Okay. Here is an open room. Let me know if you need anything.
Customer: Yes. Thank you.
Retail Clerk: The cash register is over here *when/if* you're ready to check out.

Alteration

Customer: Excuse me. These pants are too small. Is there a *bigger* size? I couldn't find it on the sales rack.
Retail Clerk: No. I'm sorry. Those come in one size only.

Customer: Excuse me. This shirt is too big. Is there a smaller size? I couldn't find it on the sales rack.
Retail Clerk: Yes. Please wait and I'll go check in the stockroom.
Customer: Okay. Thanks a lot.

Retail Clerk: No. I'm sorry we are out of stock. We don't have it here, but you could check at another <u>Summer's</u>.

Purchasing Items

Retail Clerk: I can take those for you.
Customer: I will keep these two. I don't want this one.
Retail Clerk: Okay. The cash register is over here when you're ready to check out.

Upselling

Retail Clerk: That dress looks great on you! We have some flat shoes that would go with that. Would you like to see them?
Customer: Yes, I would. Thank you very much!

Role play

In groups of 3, practice the 5 situations. Alternate roles for each situation.

1. Customer comes into the fitting room.
2. Customer wants a bigger size but it is one size only.
3. Customer wants another size but it is out of stock. Tell them to check another Zara.
4. Customer is finished trying on items.
5. Upsell 2 items while customer is trying on jeans.

Lesson 11
Dealing with Reservations & Transfers

Vocabulary

product number
reserve
reservation
reservation list
pick up
business hours

display window

Key Phrases

What would you like to reserve?
What is the product number?
Let me check and call you back.
I will reserve it for you.
Our business hours are *9am* to *10pm*.

Practice Dialogues

Customer Wants a Reservation for Item By Phone (for tomorrow)

Customer: Hi. Can I reserve an item, please?
Retail Clerk: Yes. What is the product number?
Customer: It is HYW7485.
Retail Clerk: No. I'm sorry that's out of stock.
Customer: Could you check another one? The product number is GQX7364.
Retail Clerk: Yes. That one is in stock. I will reserve it for you.

Retail Clerk: 안녕하세요. 써머스입니다. (Hello, this is Summer's)
Customer: Oh, excuse me. Do you speak English?
Retail Clerk: Yes, I do. How may I help you?
Customer: Could I make a reservation for an item to pick up tomorrow?
Retail Clerk: Yes, that's no problem. What would you like to reserve?

Customer: I'd like to reserve a *shirt* in your classic collection. I saw it on the internet.
Retail Clerk: Okay, no problem. Let me check and call you back. What is your name and telephone number?
Customer: My name is *David Hoff*. My phone number is *010-4567-8765*.
Retail Clerk: Okay. Good bye.

Retail Clerk calls customer back.
Retail Clerk: Hi. This is <u>Summer's</u> in *Gang-nam*. We have the shirt in stock. I'll reserve it for you. We can't keep a reservation longer than one day, so please come before we close tomorrow
Customer: Okay. I will. What are your business hours?
Retail Clerk: We are open from *11am* to *10pm*.
Customer: Okay. I'll be there tomorrow. Thank you so much.
Retail Clerk: Thank you. Goodbye.

Customer Wants a Reservation for an Item By Phone (in 1 week, not allowed)

Retail Clerk: How may I help you?
Customer: Could I make a reservation for an item to pick up next week?
Retail Clerk: Oh, no. I'm very sorry. We can only take reservations until the next business day. You can call back later if you'd like.
Customer: Oh, okay. I'll try to call back then.
Retail Clerk: I'm sorry about that. Have a nice day. Goodbye.

Customer: I want to make a reservation for your new leather pants shipment next week.

Retail Clerk: No. I'm sorry. We can only take reservations to be picked up in one day.
Customer: Why not? I know they will be sold quickly.
Retail Clerk: I'm very sorry. You can call when we get the shipment and we can reserve it for you then.

Reservation for Item in Display window
(Put Customer on the Reservation List)

Customer: Hi, I couldn't find the item on your display window.
Retail Clerk: Yes, I'm very sorry. That item is out of stock. I could put you on the reservation list for that item if you'd like. We usually change the window once a month.
Customer: Yes, that would be great. Thanks!
Retail Clerk: Sometimes there is a slight color change of the items because of the bright lights. Is that okay?
Customer: Hmm... well, I will look at them first when you call me.

Transfers (Transfers to Other Stores are Not Allowed)

Customer: Hi, do you have this item in large?
Retail Clerk: No. I'm so sorry. It's out of stock.
Customer: Well, could you order the item from another store?
Retail Clerk: No. We cannot transfer items from another store because of Summer's policy. There are a few other stores in Busan. I can call them to see if they have it, but you will need to go there.
Customer: Hmm.... That's pretty inconvenient for me.

Retail Clerk: Yes, I'm so sorry about that. Would you like me to call for you?
Customer: Yes, please.

Retail Clerk: Your item is available at the Summer's in Seomyeon. And I wrote down the item number for you. Please, show this to them.
Customer: Ok. Thank you for your help.

Role Play

Practice in partners. If possible, use phone to help act out the situation.

1. Customer wants a transfer from another store. Apologize and offer to call and give item number.
2. Customer wants to make a reservation for an item by phone (to pick up **tomorrow**).
3. Customer wants to make a reservation for an item by phone (to pick up in **one week**).
4. Customer is interested in display window item. But it is out of stock.
5. Customer wants to make a reservation for an item (during off-season).

Lesson 12
Dealing With Exchanges/Refunds

Vocabulary

exchange
receipt
refund
return
take off/took off/taken off (remove clothing)

Key Phrases

Do you have your receipt?
What *size/color* would you like to exchange it for?
I can't exchange this because the sales tag has been removed.
Why are you returning it?

Customer Questions

I need to exchange these *pants*.
I would like to *return* it.

Practice Dialogues

Customer: Excuse me. I bought this last week but it's too small. I would like to exchange it.
Retail Clerk: Do you have your receipt?
Customer: Yes, I do here it is.
Retail Clerk: Let me see for you. What size would you like to exchange it for?
Customer: I need a size bigger, please.
Retail Clerk: Yes, no problem. I will get that for you.

Customer: I need to exchange this shirt.
Retail Clerk: Can I see your receipt?
Customer: I don't have it.
Retail Clerk: I'm sorry. I can't exchange an item if you don't have the receipt.

Customer: Excuse me. I want to exchange this to a different color.
Retail Clerk: Do you have the receipt?
Customer: Yes.
Retail Clerk: I'm sorry but I can't exchange this since the sales tag has been taken off.

Customer: Excuse me. I need to refund an item.
Retail Clerk: That should be no problem. Do you have your receipt?
Customer: Yes. Here it is.
Retail: Oh, I'm very sorry but you bought this 2 months ago. We cannot exchange items more than 30 days after the purchase.

Customer: I want to exchange this.
Retail Clerk: Lets see. Do you have the receipt?
Customer: Yes. Here it is.
Retail Clerk: That's no problem. Why are you returning it?
Customer: It was a gift from my boyfriend.
Retail Clerk: Oh, okay. I understand. Here is your money. Have a wonderful day!

Role Play Practice

In pairs, practice the situations.

1. Customer wants an exchange but is missing the receipt.
2. Customer wants an exchange and has receipt and sales tag.
3. Customer wants to return an item and has receipt and sales tag.
4. Customer wants to return an item but it is over 30 days since the purchase.
5. Customer wants to return an item but it is missing the sales tag.

Chapter 13
Alterations

Vocabulary

alteration
sleeves
shortened/lengthened
fee
measurements

Key Phrases

You will need to pay an alteration fee.
It will take about a week.
Let me take your measurements.
Could you show me how you'd like the length?
I will give you a call, so you can come pick it up.

Practice Dialogues

Customer wants an Alteration

Customer: Excuse me. This blazer sleeves are a bit too long. Can they be shortened?
Retail Clerk: Yes, that should be no problem. You will need to pay an alteration fee and it will take about a week. Is that okay?
Customer: Yes. That's okay with me.
Retail Clerk: Let me take your measurements at the mirror.
Continued
Retail Clerk: Please, stand straight facing the mirror. Could you show me how you'd like the length?
Customer: I want it a few centimeters shorter on the sleeves.
Retail Clerk: How's this?
Customer: A little bit shorter than that.
Retail Clerk: How's this?
Customer: Perfect!
Retail Clerk: Please, check the length one more time, looking at the mirror.
Customer: Actually that is a bit too short.
Retail Clerk: How's this?
Customer: That is good. Thanks.

Retail Clerk: Let me get your name and telephone number.
Customer: My name is *Tom Smith*. My phone number is *010-111-1111*
Retail Clerk: After the alteration, we can't take any exchanges or refunds. Is that okay?
Customer: That's okay.
Retail Clerk: It will take about a week to change. I will give you a call then so you can come pick it up.
Customer: Okay. Thank you. Talk to you then.
Retail Clerk: Thank you. Have a nice day.

Role Play Practice

Each student brings a tape measure to class. Find a partner. Use the wall as a "mirror." Practice customer and clerk suggesting and requesting an alteration.

Lesson 14
Recommending/Suggesting Clothing

Key Phrases

Would you like to see them?
Would you like to take a look at our new *skirts*?
We have a new selection of *sweaters*.

Would you like to see our *Winter/Fall* collection?
The *t-shirts* are on sale today.
Take a look if you'd like.
This is very fashionable these days.
These *shoes* go well with these *pants*.
Just to let you know.
We have some similar *styles* in different *colors*.

Practice Dialogues

Customer: Do you have leather shoes?
Retail Clerk: No. But we have a new selection of dress shoes. Would you like to see them?
Customer: Yes. Okay. I will take a look.

Show customer styles that you believe they would like.

Customer: I'm looking for a pair of pants like I saw in your catalog. They were neon green. Do you have them?
Retail Clerk: Do you know the product number?
Customer: It's GBC4637.
Retail Clerk: No. I'm really sorry. It's out of stock. That was last year's collection. This year we have a new selection of leather pants that I think you would like. Would you like to see?
Customer: Okay. That sounds good.

Recommend clothing for a gift (father to daughter)

Retail Clerk: Hello. Can I help you find something today?
Customer: Yes. I'm shopping for my daughter. I really don't know what I'm looking for.

Retail Clerk: Okay. Let me help you. How old is she?

Customer: She's in her 20's.
Retail Clerk: Do you think she'd like this skirt? They are very fashionable these days.
Customer: I think she'd like that.
Retail Clerk: Can you show me something else?
Customer: Sure. These shoes are also popular. They go excellent together with this skirt.

Recommend other items to go with an item the customer has tried on in the fitting room

Retail Clerk: That sweater looks great on you. We have some washed jeans that would look great with those.
Customer: Okay. Could you show them to me, please?
Retail Clerk: No, problem. What size do you wear? I'll get them for you.
Customer: I wear a 32.

Role Play

List 5 different items from your store. Find a partner and complete the 4 situations using your list.

1. Recommend items to a browsing customer.
2. Recommend items for a mom shopping for her daughter.
3. Upsell items after customer tried on items in the fitting room.
4. Upsell items to a customer at the cash register.

Lesson 15
Handling Difficult
Customers

Key Phrases

I'm very sorry.
I'm so sorry.
It's *Summer's* policy.
There is nothing I can do.
I'm sorry for the inconvenience.

Please understand, sir/ma'am.

*Understanding Some Cultural Differences

*Ignoring an angry customer can make the customer more
angry.
*Be careful not to show any physical contact during an
argument.
*Be careful about speaking your native language to
colleagues in front of the customer.

Group discussion: Share stories about difficult customers
you have had. What was the problem? How did you deal
with the situation?

Nagging Customer

Customer: Do you have these blue pants?
Retail Clerk: No. I'm so sorry. It's out of stock.
Customer: But I saw it here two days ago.
Retail Clerk: I'm sorry. We receive a different shipment each week.
Customer: That's strange. I don't understand why you do that.
Retail Clerk: I'm sorry for the inconvenience.

Customer wants to transfer an item from another store.

Customer: Excuse me. Do you have this pants in a size 32?
Retail Clerk: No, I'm sorry. It's out of stock.
Customer: Then, can you transfer it from another store?
Retail Clerk: No, we can't do transfers at <u>Summer's</u>.
Customer: Can you just do it this time? I'm really busy and I can't go somewhere else.
Retail Clerk: I'm really sorry. It's <u>Summer's</u> policy. There's nothing I can do.

Angry Customer

Customer: Where is the bathroom?
Retail Clerk: There is no bathroom in the store.
Customer: What do you mean no bathroom?! This is crazy!
Retail Clerk: I'm so sorry.

Customer is angry about not being able to return an item.

Customer: I would like to return this.
Retail Clerk: Do you have your receipt?
Customer: No. I don't have it. Isn't it okay?

Retail Clerk: No. I'm sorry but you can't return an item without the receipt.
Customer: What do you mean I can't? I paid for this and I want to return it!
Retail Clerk: I'm very sorry, sir. But I can't return this item for you because you don't have a receipt. It's Summer's policy.
Customer: What the #$%&! I'm never shopping at Summer's again! This is so stupid!
Retail Clerk: Again, I'm very sorry, sir. Have a nice day.

Dissatisfied Customer

Customer: Where are the sale items?
Retail Clerk: I'm sorry. We aren't having a sale now.
Customer: No sale?! But all of these pants were on sale yesterday.
Retail Clerk: Yes. I'm so sorry. The sale has finished. There's nothing I can do.

Customer wants an item but it is out of stock.

Customer: Excuse me. Do you have these pants? I saw them here last week but I can't find them.
Retail Clerk: I'm sorry, but those pants are out of stock.
Customer: What do you mean they are out of stock? I just saw them here last week.
Retail Clerk: I'm sorry about that. We get a new shipment every two weeks. I can call another store to ask if it is available for you.
Customer: Yes, okay that sounds good. Thank you.

Role Play

Practice nagging, angry, and dissatisfied customer situations with your partner.

Dealing WIth Complaints

Activity: Think with your partner. What are 4 types of complaints a customer may have?
How can you resolve these problems?

1. Problem:

_____

Solution:

_____

2. Problem:

_____

Solution:

_____

3. Problem:

_____

Solution:

_____

4. Problem:

_____

Solution:

_____

Vocabulary

replace
tear/tore/torn
charge

Key Phrases

I'm very sorry about this.
We will fix it.
We will try our best to fix it.
We will try and correct this.
The only thing we can do is replace it.
We can replace it.

Practice Dialogues

Customer: These pants tore the first day after I bought them.
Retail Clerk: I'm very sorry about this. The only thing we can do is replace it. Is that okay?

Customer: On my receipt, you charged_me $20 more.
Retail Clerk: I'm sorry about that. I will correct it for you.

Role Play

Practice the complaint situations you wrote at the beginning of the lesson with a partner. Use the new phrases/vocabulary you learned.

Lesson 16
Acknowledging the Customer

Key Phrases

What can I help you with today?
If you need any help today, please let me know.
Please let me know if there is anything I can help you with.
The *classic t-shirts* are buy one get one free.
We are having a sale this week. Take a look if you are interested.
Excuse me. Do you need help?

You look like you need help.
If there something I can help you with?
Hello. This is *Summer's* in *Mumbai Department Store* . How may I help you?
Yes. This is *Summer's*. This is *Yoo-jung* speaking. How may I help you?

Practice Dialogues

Greeting Customer

Retail Clerk: Welcome to <u>Summer's</u>. Thank you for coming in today. Let me know if I can help you with anything.
Customer: Thank you. I will.

Retail Clerk: Hello. How are you today? What can I help you with today?
Customer: Hi. I'm just looking. Thank you.

Retail Clerk: Welcome to <u>Summer's</u>. Let me know if there's anything I can help you with.
Customer: Okay. I will. Thank you.

Promotions

Retail Clerk: We are having a special promotion this week. If you buy 2 classic t-shirts, you can get one free.
Customer: Thank you. That sounds great.

Retail Clerk: Hi. I just wanted to tell you that all of these shirts are on sale today.
Customer: Okay. Thank you for telling me.

Customer Appears to Need Help/Be frustrated

Retail Clerk: Excuse me. Do you need any help?
Customer: Yes. I can't find a large size.
Retail Clerk: Let me check if there is one in the stockroom. Just a moment, please.

Retail Clerk: You look like you need help.
Customer: Yes. I can't find the dress I saw here last week.
Retail Clerk: What did it look like?

Answering the Phone

Ringing
Retail Clerk: 안녕하세요. (Hello?)
Customer: I'm sorry. I don't speak Korean.

Retail Clerk: This is the <u>Summer's </u>in Seomyeon. My name is Han-song. How may I help you?
Customer: I was wondering what your business hours are.
Retail Clerk: We are open from 11am to 10pm.
Customer: Thank you.
Retail Clerk: Thank you. Have a nice day.

Retail Clerk: This is Hye-eun at <u>Summer's</u>. What can I do for you?
Customer: I want to know if you have some shoes I saw on your website.
Retail Clerk: Do you know their product number?
Customer: Yes. It is HDB8237.
Retail Clerk: Let me check.

Activity

One student goes to the whiteboard as the "artist." The other students, sitting down, are the "describers." The teacher shows the describers a picture of people with a variety of facial expressions. The describers describe the picture to the artist. The artist draws what the describers explain.

Lesson 17
Checking Customer Needs

Vocabulary

in particular
goes with something

Key Phrases

How do you like this *dress*?
What are you looking for today?
What kind of style are you interested in?
What do you think about this?
Are you looking for anything in particular?

Practice Dialogues

Retail Clerk: What are you looking for today?
Customer: I'm looking for a sweater.
Retail Clerk: We have some sweaters over here. What do you think about these?
Customer: Yes. I like them.

Retail Clerk: Are you looking for anything <u>in particular</u>?
Customer: Yes. I'm looking for some pants for a party.
Retail Clerk: What kind of style are you interested in?
Customer: I'd like something cute and bright.
Retail Clerk: What do you think about this?
Customer: It's good but I don't think it would look good on me.
Retail Clerk: That's okay. You can try it on and see. How about this?
Customer: Yes. I like that a lot. I'll try it on.

Activity

Pictionary game. The teacher secretly gives a customer question to one student. The student must *draw* the sentence on the whiteboard. The other students try to guess the customer's question. *The first words of the question may be given as hints.

Lesson 18
Handling Emergencies

List together different types of emergencies:

1. _____

2. _____

3._____

4._____

5._____

Vocabulary

faint
evacuation
evacuate
belongings

Key Phrases

It's an emergency.
Don't panic.
This is an evacuation.
We are evacuating.
You need to evacuate/ leave the building.
Please, do not forget your belongings.
I will call 911.
We called 911.
Someone is coming.

Practice Dialogues

Medical Emergency

Customer: My friend fainted! I can't wake him up.
Retail Clerk: I will call 911. Someone is coming.

Customer: My father is having trouble breathing. Please, call 911.
Retail Clerk: We called 911. Someone is coming.

Fire

Retail Clerk: There is a fire! Please, evacuate the building.
Customer: Yes. I understand.

Customer: Why is the alarm ringing?
Retail Clerk: There is a fire. You need to leave the building.

Store Evacuation

Retail Clerk: I'm sorry, but you need to evacuate the building. Its an emergency.
Customer: What's wrong?
Retail Clerk: I don't know. Please, leave the building quickly.

Eric Thomas

ABOUT THE AUTHOR

Eric has taught English for large corporations and individuals, both abroad and within the US. For more information about Eric, view: www.linkedin.com/in/ethomas8.

15772274R00050

Printed in Poland
by Amazon Fulfillment
Poland Sp. z o.o., Wrocław